The Masks We Wore

A Pandemic Picture Book

Written by Freeman Ng

Illustrated by Juliana Castro, Jessica Chrysler. Rebecca Hoenig, Ruby Michelle, Sara Nintzel, Alicia Schwab, Eshanthie Tyner, Cheryl Ann Warren, and Brigitte West

ISBN: 978-0-9906197-9-6

www.PandemicPB.com

Three Daughters Press
www.ThreeDaughtersPress.com

These are the masks that we wore for each other.

These are the distances we kept
To stop the virus from jumping the gaps,

And the masks that we wore for each other.

These are the gatherings we skipped for the sake
Of the people we love whose danger was great,

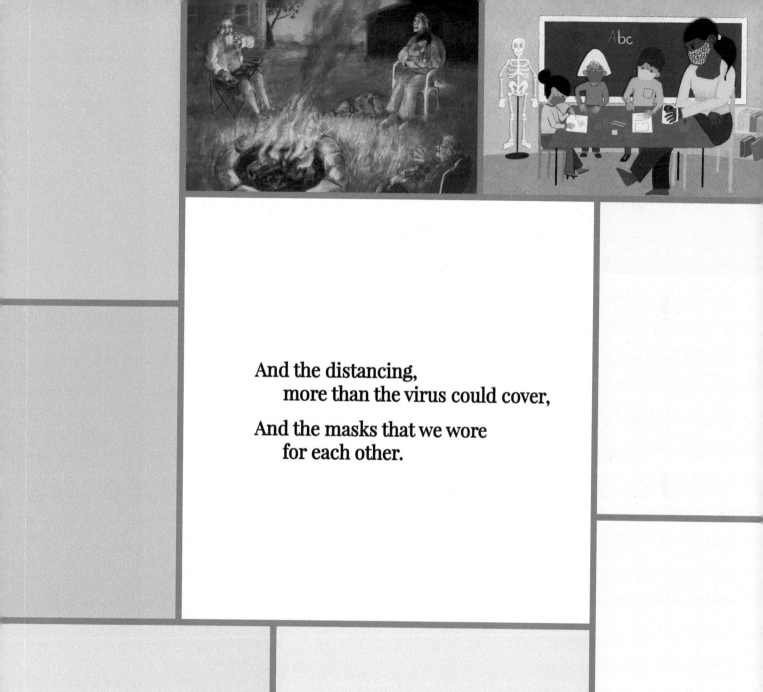

And the distancing,
    more than the virus could cover,

And the masks that we wore
    for each other.

These are the workers whose jobs were so vital,
Supplying the goods that we'd need for survival,

And the gatherings we skipped
    for the people we treasure,

And the distancing,
    more than the virus could cover,

And the masks that we wore
    for each other.

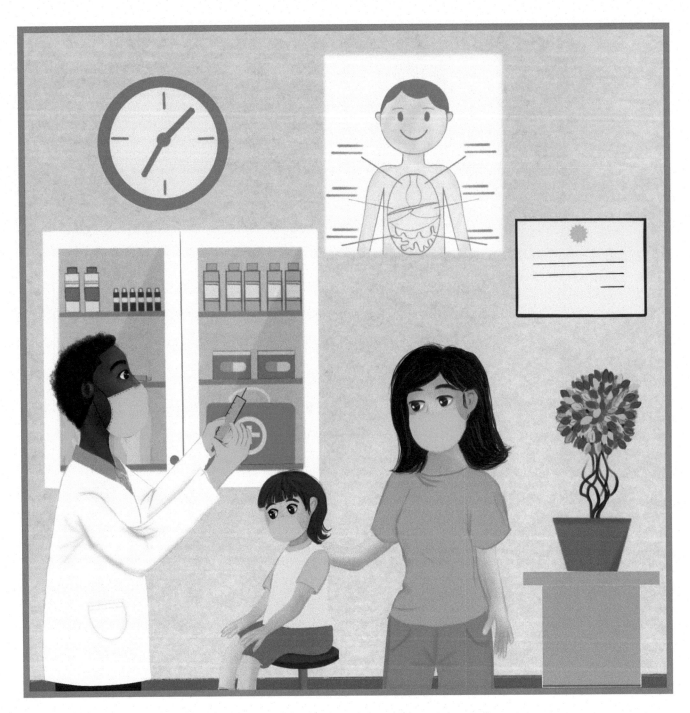

These are the doctors and nurses who
Tested and treated and carried us through,

And the workers who did
so much more than their share,

And the gatherings we skipped
for the people we treasure,

And the distancing,
more than the virus could cover,

And the masks that we wore
for each other.

These are the scientists, some of the brightest,
Who made the vaccines that would fend off the virus,

And the doctors and nurses
who gave us our care,

And the workers who did
so much more than their share,

And the gatherings we skipped
for the people we treasure,

And the distancing,
more than the virus could cover,

And the masks that we wore
for each other.

These are the leaders who fought for the people,
Who warned us and taught us and led by example,

And the scientists working,
   vaccines to prepare,

And the doctors and nurses
   who gave us our care,

And the workers who did
   so much more than their share,

And the gatherings we skipped
   for the people we treasure,

And the distancing,
   more than the virus could cover,

And the masks that we wore
   for each other.

This is the day we walked out of our homes
And hugged once again the world we had known,

Thanks to our leaders
who guided us there,

And the scientists working,
vaccines to prepare,

And the doctors and nurses
who gave us our care,

And the workers who did
so much more than their share,

And the gatherings we skipped
for the people we treasure,

And the distancing,
more than the virus could cover,

And the troubles we took
and the pains we endured...

And the masks that we wore

for each other.

The Battle

Sheltering in our homes is one of the ways we're fighting against the Covid virus, but that's not all we're doing.

We wear masks to keep ourselves from breathing in too much of the virus, or breathing out too much of it if we have it. The masks don't totally prevent the virus from getting into the air or into our bodies, but they help to slow it down.

We also keep our distance, so the virus has farther to go in order to pass from one person to another. Distancing doesn't keep us totally out of the reach of the virus, but it helps to slow it down.

Slowing down the virus gave us time to create vaccines that train our bodies to better fight it off. The vaccines don't totally prevent us from catching the virus, but they make it less likely. They also keep us from getting as sick as we might if we do catch the virus.

Today, in the year 2023, Covid is still with us, but it's not as bad as it could be. Many, many people, maybe even you or me, have been saved from getting seriously sick or worse by the sheltering in place we've done, the vaccinations we've received, the distances we've kept, and the masks we've worn.

Author

Freeman Ng is the author of *Basho's Haiku Journeys*, a haiku picture book, *Who Am I?*, a personalizable picture book, and the forthcoming *Bridge Across The Sky* (Simon & Schuster, 2024) a Young Adult novel-in-verse about the Chinese immigration experience through Angel Island in the early 1900's.

www.AuthorFreeman.com

Illustrators

Juliana Castro is a Colombian illustrator and Visual Development artist based in Florida. She creates digital and traditional illustrations for children's books and animation.

Her work portrays animals, environments, and diverse characters. With her work, she strives to raise awareness about these topics, while bringing a smile to your face!

www.JulianaCastrC.com

Jessica Chrysler is a fantasy artist and writer from California. Born in the big city of LA, her work is inspired by her wanderings of nature and love of gothic fairytales. While painting pictures for kids gives her the greatest joy, she also creates art for comics and video games.

www.JessChrysler.com

Haley Grunloh is an artist from New Haven, CT. She has taught drawing, cartooning, and other very important skills to adults and children of all ages at Creative Arts Workshop, IS183 Art School of the Berkshires, and the New Haven Free Public Library.

www.HaleyGrunloh.com

Rebecca Jane Hoenig is a lifelong book lover and artist. Growing up in a family of English professors, surrounded by mountains of books, oodles of paper and pencils, it is inevitable that she would want to make her own books. She won the Fall/Winter 2022 SCBWI Eastern PA Banner Competition.

www.RebeccaJaneHoenig.com

Annie Kuhn was teaching at a college in NY when the pandemic hit. She switched to teaching online, missing her students terribly. Now living in St. Paul, Minnesota, Annie is freelance artist, writer, and editor. Annie has two cats, two grown daughters, one husband, and far too many art supplies!

www.AnnieKuhnCreates.com

Ruby Michelle is an illustrator from Elk Grove, California. She is currently studying in the Children's Book Illustration Program at UC San Diego and is working towards publishing her first children's book. Ruby's works are inspired by Asian culture, nature and daily life and her art has been exhibited throughout California.

https://www.RubyMichelle.com

Sara Nintzel Illustrated her first picture book, The (Mis) Adventures of Dasher, about unconditional love, in 2020. She's finishing her second book, Wonderful Being: Positive Affirmations for Kids, with illustrated forest animals, to launch in 2023. She lives in St. Paul, Minnesota, with her husband, three sons and two dogs.

www.SaraNintzel.com

Olivia Pinney is a student who possesses a love for traditional and illustrative art and writing. She won a regional award in the 2021 Scholastic Art and Writing competition. Her work has been published in several literary journals, literary magazines and children's books.

www.scbwi.org/illustrator-gallery/illustrator-detail/?
illustrator_id=84113

A recently graduated art major, **Wendy Roble's** work focuses on the fantastic, surreal, and the horrific, with emphasis on exploring iconography. They love the idea of being a book illustrator, and their freelancing career would be off to a much smoother start if their cat didn't try to eat their supplies.

RedBeanCarp.carrd.co

Alicia Schwab was raised in southern Wisconsin by two eccentric bookworms. She started making books when she was little and has gone on to illustrate books and publications in Germany and the States including: THE MUKLUK BALL, TAKOZA, LITE, Ladybug Magazine and more forthcoming titles.

www.AliciaSchwab.com

Eshanthie Tyner is an illustrator based in Maryland. During the pandemic, she tried her hand at digital art, and it quickly became her passion. Her art features portraits of children from around the world. She currently teaches and enjoys spending her free time with her daughter, mom, and three sisters.

Gabriela Vega is a proud Latina children's book illustrator from Southern California. She is the illustrator for *Cactus Dance*, written by April Lesher and *I Love You My Little Taquito* written by Naibe Reynoso. When she's not illustrating, she enjoys spending time with her dog Mumu and drawing in her sketchbook

www.GabrielaVegaArt.com

Cheryl Ann Warren is a children's book illustrator. She was born and raised in Zimbabwe, to a Ukrainian mom and Zimbabwean dad. Today (and during the Covid 19 pandemic), she lives in beautiful Kansas City with her husband, their children and of course the boss of the whole show, their cat, Luna.

www.CherylAnnWarren.com

Brigitte West is a writer and artist, whose love for story-telling led to illustration freelancing. Their work has appeared in Taproot Magazine and been featured on album covers, greeting cards, and more! Currently, Brigitte is working on a children's book. They live in Midcoast Maine with their cat, Ramona.

www.BrigitteWest.com

Illustrator credits for *The Masks We Wore*

- "15.3" means page 15, illustration #3, "12" means the sole large illustration on page 12.

- Page numbers start with the first page of the story. (Third page of the book.)

- For pages with multiple framed illustrations, the illustrations are numbered starting with the one at the top center and going clockwise.

- For pages with free-floating illustrations, illustrations are numbered starting at the top left.

Juliana Castro: 15.1
Jessica Chrysler: 2, 9.2, 13.1
Rebecca Hoenig: 1, 9.3, 11.1, 13.4, 14, 17.1
Ruby Michelle: 17.7
Sara Nintzel: 9.1
Alicia Schwab: 6, 7.1, 7.2, 9.4, 11.2, 12, 13.5, 13.6, 15.6, 16.2
Eshanthie Tyner: 3.1, 7.3, 8, 11.3, 13.3, 16.5, 17.4, 17.6
Cheryl Ann Warren: 4, 5.2, 10, 11.4, 11.5, 13.2, 15.2, 15.4, 15.5, 16.1, 16.3, 16.4, 16.6, 17.2, 17.5
Brigitte West: 5.1, 15.3, 17.3

Illustrator credits for *The House We Sheltered In*

- "15.3" means page 15, illustration #3, "12" means the sole large illustration on page 12.

- Page numbers start with the first page of the story. (Third page of the book.)

- For pages with multiple framed illustrations, the illustrations are numbered starting with the one at the top center and going clockwise.

- For pages with free-floating illustrations, illustrations are numbered starting at the top left.

 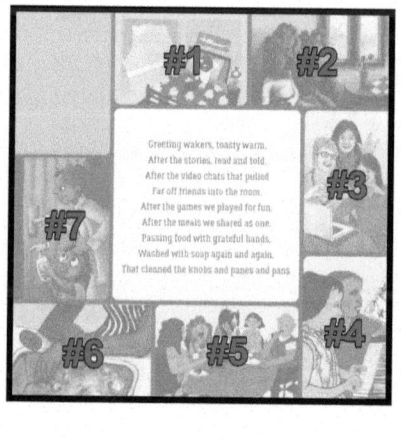 

Alicia Schwab: 5.1, 6, 11.3, 13.1, 13.4, 13.5, 13.6, 15.2, 15.3, 15.4, 18.6

Annie Kuhn: 9.2, 12, 17.3, 18.1

Brigitte West: 9.1, 11.1, 14, 18.3

Cheryl Ann Warren: cover, 1, 8, 9.3, 13.2, 17.1, 17.5, 18.2, 18.4

Eshanthie Tyner: 7.2

Gabriela Vega: 15.1

Haley Grunloh: 5.2, 17.7

Jessica Chrysler: 4, 18.5

Juliana Castro: 2, 3.1, 7.1, 7.3, 11.5, 19.1

Rebecca Hoenig: 10, 15.6, 15.7, 17.4, 17.6, 19.3

Ruby Michelle: 13.3, 19.5

Sara Nintzel: title page, 9.4, 11.4, 15.5, 19.2, 19.4

Olivia Pinney: 11.2

Wendy Roble: 16, 17.2

The Virus

In the year 2020, we began getting sick from a new virus, which we named Covid.

A virus is a small bit of the material that living things are made of, smaller than any germ, way too small to see without a very powerful microscope. Just like germs, they can get inside the bodies of living things and make them sick.

Covid can make us very, very sick, and it spreads mostly through the air. When someone who has the virus breathes out, the virus floats out into the air along with their breath. Then, if others breathe in enough of it, they might catch it as well.

To protect ourselves from the virus and keep ourselves from passing it to others, we began "sheltering in place," staying home as much as we could.

This is hard for some people, but it isn't all bad. After all, home can be a nice place to be. For many, it's where they can always find the people they love the most.

we sheltered in.

Of all the homes

Greeting wakers, toasty warm,
After the stories, read and told,
After the video chats that pulled
Far off friends into the room,
After the games we played for fun,
After the meals we shared as one,
Passing food with grateful hands,
Washed with soap again and again,
That cleaned the knobs and panes and pans

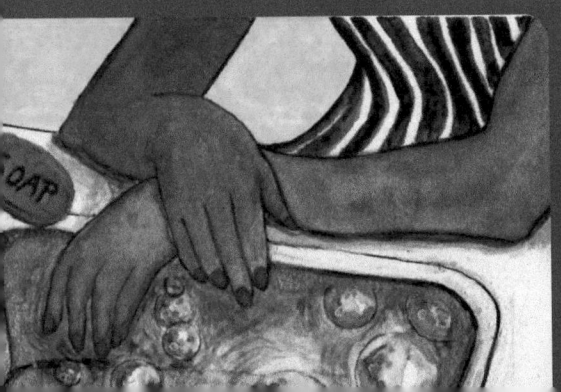
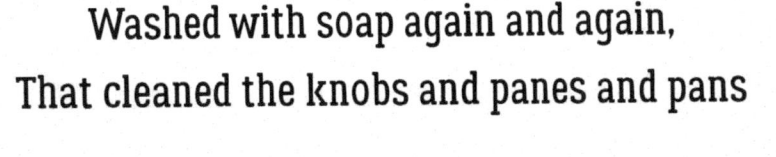

This is yet another dawn,

After the stories, read and told,
After the video chats that pulled
Far off friends into the room,
After the games we played for fun,
After the meals we shared as one,
Passing food with grateful hands,
Washed with soap again and again,
That cleaned the knobs and panes and pans
Of the house we sheltered in.

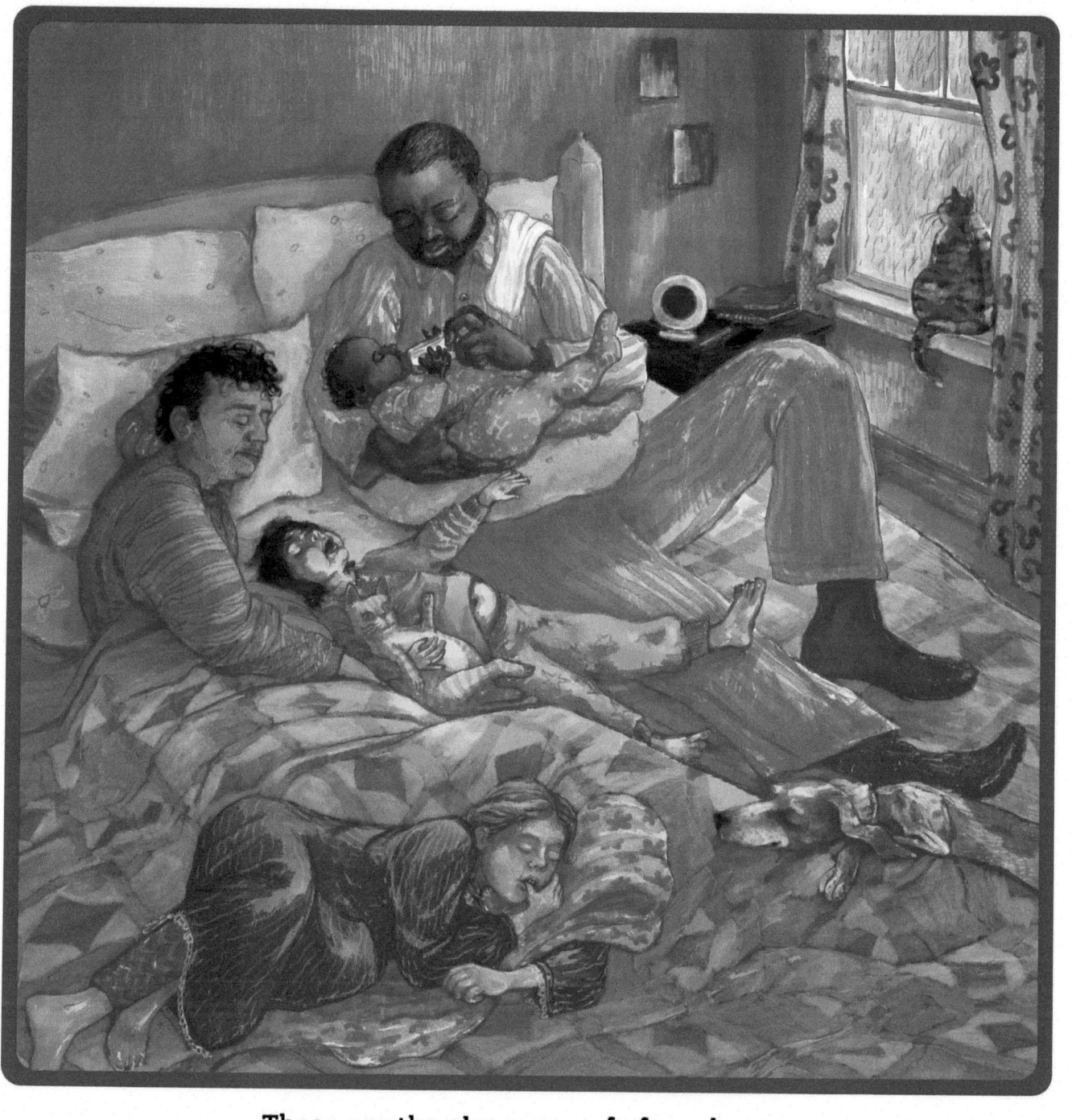

These are the sleepers, safe from harm,

After the video chats that pulled
Far off friends into the room,
After the games we played for fun,
After the meals we shared as one,
Passing food with grateful hands,
Washed with soap again and again,
That cleaned the knobs and panes and pans
Of the house we sheltered in.

These are the stories, read and told,

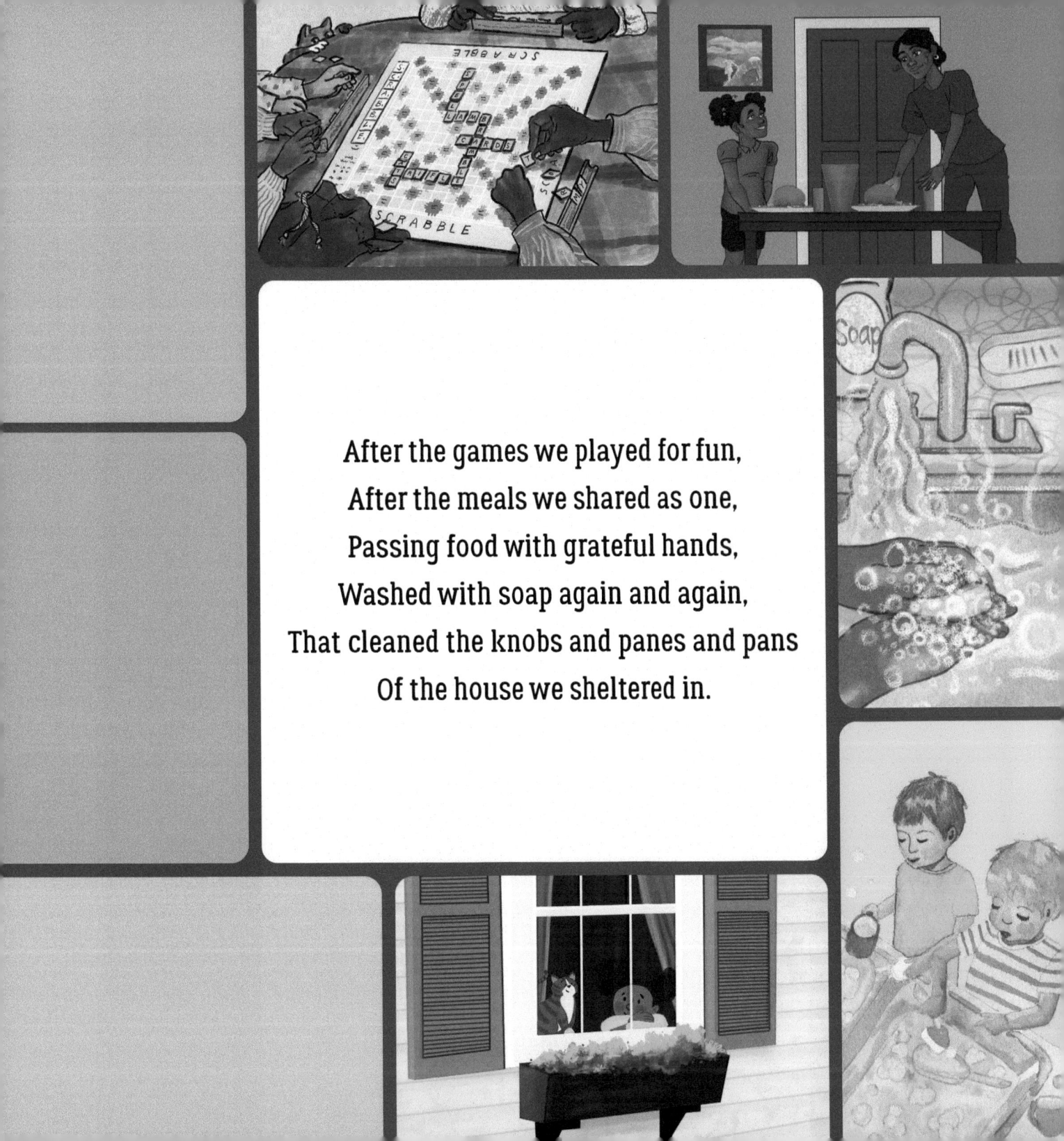

After the games we played for fun,
After the meals we shared as one,
Passing food with grateful hands,
Washed with soap again and again,
That cleaned the knobs and panes and pans
Of the house we sheltered in.

These are the video chats that pulled
Far off friends into the room,

After the meals we shared as one,
Passing food with grateful hands,
Washed with soap again and again,
That cleaned the knobs and panes and pans
Of the house we sheltered in.

These are the games we played for fun,

Washed with soap again and again,
That cleaned the knobs and panes and pans
Of the house we sheltered in.

These are the meals we shared as one,
Passing food with grateful hands,

That cleaned the knobs and panes and pans
Of the house we sheltered in.

This is the soap that washed the hands,
Again and again, and again and again,

Of the house we sheltered in.

These are the hands, nimble and strong,
That cleaned the knobs and panes and pans

This is the house we sheltered in.

The House We Sheltered In

A Pandemic Picture Book

Written by Freeman Ng

Illustrated by Alicia Schwab, Annie Kuhn, Brigitte West, Cheryl Ann Warren, Eshanthie Tyner, Gabriela Vega, Haley Grunloh, Jessica Chrysler, Juliana Castro, Rebecca Hoenig, Ruby Michelle, Sara Nintzel, Olivia Pinney, and Wendy Roble

ISBN: 978-0-9906197-9-6

www.PandemicPB.com

Three Daughters Press
www.ThreeDaughtersPress.com